F

HOW THEY MADE THINGS WORK!
IN TUDOR AND STUART TIMES

Written by Richard Platt • Illustrated by David Lawrence

W
FRANKLIN WATTS
LONDON•SYDNEY

First published in 2008 by Franklin Watts

Text copyright © Richard Platt 2008
Illustrations copyright © Franklin Watts 2008

Franklin Watts
338 Euston Road
London NW1 3BH

Franklin Watts Australia
Level 17/207 Kent Street
Sydney NSW 2000

A CIP catalogue record is available from the British Library.

Dewey number: 609

ISBN 978 0 7496 7481 6

Printed in China

Franklin Watts is a division of Hachette Children's Books,
an Hachette Livre UK company.
www.hachettelivre.co.uk

Art Director Jonathan Hair
Editor in Chief John C. Miles
Designer Matthew Lilly
Editor Sarah Ridley
Picture researcher Sarah Smithies

Picture credits:
Ancient Art & Architecture Collection: 15, 28; CNAM, Paris / Lauros
/ Giraudon / The Bridgeman Art Library: 19; Mary Evans Picture
Library: 12; NASA / JPL / University of Arizona: 8; National Gallery,
London / The Bridgeman Art Library: 20; PRISMA / Ancient Art &
Architecture Collection: 9, 21; Science Museum: 23; Skyscan /
Corbis : 7, Back Cover; Stapleton Collection / Corbis: 17; The
Bridgeman Art Library: 16; The Print Collector / Alamy: 11;
Topfoto: 27; World History Archive / TopFoto: 24.

Contents

How they made things work
in Tudor and Stuart times 4

Firearms 6

Telescope 8

Microscope 10

Clocks 12

Printing 14

Navigation 16

Thermometer 18

Oil paint 20

Water closet 22

Arithmetic.....................24

Knitting machine 26

Distilled alcohol 28

Glossary/websites 30

Index 32

HOW THEY MADE THINGS WORK IN TUDOR AND STUART TIMES

Many crucial inventions arrived in Britain from Europe during Tudor and Stuart times (1485–1714). They were a result of what historians call the Renaissance – some 300 years of learning, experiment and discovery that began in Italy in the 14th century.

Rediscovering ancient wisdom

Meaning "rebirth", the Renaissance started when scholars took renewed interest in the forgotten knowledge of ancient Greece and Rome. They also studied the wisdom and technology of the Arab world and of India and China. However, ideas from long ago and far away were just the start. The Renaissance soon became an age of enquiry and discovery. Brilliant people from Italy to Britain started to question everything. Scientists realised that they would learn more about the world if they looked at it and measured it, instead of just arguing about it.

Printing spreads knowledge

Recorded in books, wisdom and learning were precious and rare – because books themselves were precious and rare. Monks copied them by hand, writing whole books onto calfskin with pen and ink. Even when they were complete, books meant nothing to most people because few could read. Printing changed all this. After its invention in 1439, books suddenly got cheaper. Soon there were lots of them.

With more cheap books, more people learned to read. From the neatly printed pages, they read about the exciting ideas of the Renaissance. Printed books taught people about thermometers, telescopes, microscopes and clocks, and the discoveries that scientists had made with them.

Spread by printing, Renaissance thinking transformed Europe and made the time when the Tudor and Stuart families ruled Britain one of great change.
The Renaissance helped to banish the ignorance and fixed ideas of the past.

FIREARMS

Ever since warfare began, soldiers knew they were safe behind thick walls or tough armour. These defences were strong enough to resist the biggest catapults and the sharpest swords and arrows. But then, in the 14th century, everything changed. From China came black powder: an explosive mixture of charcoal, stinking yellow sulphur and a white chemical called saltpetre. Warfare would never be the same again.

PING!

TAKE THAT!

Endless sieges

Improvements in castles and armour had made wars hard to win. Arrows just bounced off knights' plate armour and chain mail – a kind of shirt knitted from wire. The only way to capture thick-walled castles was to cut off food and water supplies, and wait for those inside to starve or surrender.

Powder and shot

Knowledge of gunpowder spread from China through the Arab world in the 13th century. By about 1325, European blacksmiths were building simple cannons. The first handguns were just like miniature cannons on sticks. These early weapons were noisy, and terrified their targets. At first they did little real damage, but they soon grew much more powerful. The new cannons could smash the walls of old-fashioned castles. Lead bullets tore through chain mail.

New castles

Gunpowder forced castle architects to change their designs. Castles became lower and walls had sloping or rounded surfaces. For instance, this castle built at Deal, England, in 1540 looks like a pattern of circles. Cannonballs bounced off the curved stones instead of doing real damage.

The flat walls of traditional castles were easy to destroy with the new firearms.

Costly firearms

Guns and powder were very costly, and 300 years passed before firearms completely replaced bows and arrows.

Gunners loaded cannons with bags of explosive gunpowder, round shot (cannonballs) and wadding to keep everything in place.

TELESCOPE

Our planet circles the Sun once a year but, until the 17th century, most people believed the opposite. They thought the Earth was the centre of the universe. What changed their minds was the invention of a Dutch optician, Hans Lippershey. He found a way to use lenses to magnify distant things. His clever device inspired a brilliant Italian stargazer, whose discoveries rearranged our view of the universe.

Limited vision

Even with the sharpest eyesight, it's hard to see far-off things clearly. Astronomers couldn't get a clear view of stars and planets. On battlefields, generals could only guess what the distant enemy was up to. At ports, merchants strained their eyes to see whether their ships were approaching.

Powerful modern telescopes allow us to view distant planets – such as Jupiter, shown here – in detail.

The "looker"

Around 1608 a Dutch spectacle-maker, Hans Lippershey (1570–1619), held two lenses some distance apart. He noticed that they enlarged a distant rooftop. Fitting them into a tube, he invented the "looker". News spread fast and within nine months, Italian scientist Galileo Galilei (1564–1642) had made his own looker, which we now call a telescope. With it he gazed at the planets, and proved that the Earth orbits the Sun.

Whose telescope?

Did Hans Lippershey really invent the telescope? He said he did but it's hard to be sure. Rival spectacle-makers, Hans and Zacharias Janssen, also claimed to be the inventors. So too did Jacob Metius, another Dutchman, and Leonard Digges of England. What's clear, though, is that Galileo was the first to use the telescope for serious astronomy.

... and the one to the right is my room!

At his workshop in Middleburg, Lippershey noticed that distant things seemed close when he lined up two different lenses: a convex (bulging out) one, and a concave (saucer-shaped) lens. His spyglass magnified things only twice. Galileo's was nearly five times more powerful.

Copernicus

Using his telescope, Galileo watched something nobody had seen before: Jupiter's moons passing in front of the planet. The only explanation for this was that both Jupiter and the Earth circle the Sun. Danish astronomer Nikolaus Copernicus (1473–1543) suggested this a century earlier, but could not prove it.

This 16th-century map of the heavens shows how Copernicus said the planets move.

MICROSCOPE

How closely can you look at something tiny? Bringing it nearer to your eye makes it bigger, but only up to a point. Move in closer and everything blurs. It wasn't until the invention of the microscope that scientists could *really* study the busy, teeming world of tiny beasts and bugs.

A water-filled glass globe was the most common kind of magnifying glass.

Magnifying matters

Our eyes can make sharp pictures only of objects bigger than about 1/25 mm – half the width of a hair from your head. This held back early scientists because many living things are smaller than this. Magnifying glasses – a 13th-century invention – helped a bit, especially when used in pairs. But none of them enlarged objects much more than about ten times.

Dutch brilliance

Dutch cloth merchant Anton van Leeuwenhoek (1632–1723) created the first really effective microscopes with lenses like water drops. His instruments were hardly bigger than postage stamps, yet they showed up objects just 1/700 mm in size.

Leeuwenhoek was the first to look at bacteria – tiny living things that spread disease.

Seen through one of the newfangled microscopes, a tiny flea looked enormous.

By magnifying snowflakes many times over, observers were able to see clearly that no two are exactly the same.

My dear Hooke, is that a spaniel flea?!

Robert Hooke

Leeuwenhoek's experiments began when he read of the work of English scientist Robert Hooke (1635–1703). Hooke used a compound (two-lens) microscope of low power. He described what he saw in a book, *Micrografia*. Hooke's microscope became so famous that England's king, Charles II, asked for a demonstration in 1663. Nevertheless, 150 years passed before compound microscopes were as good as Leeuwenhoek's simple instruments.

CLOCKS

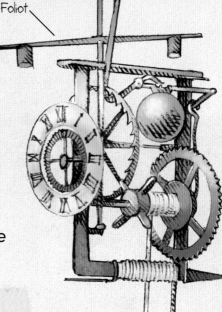

Foliot

Tick-tocking away in old houses, wind-up clocks now seem like quaint antiques. Yet 350 years ago, these brass and wood time-keepers were the very latest technology. Thanks to their pendulums (heavy swinging arms) they were 50 times more accurate than older clocks: they gained or lost no more than 10 seconds a day!

Terrible time-keepers

Early clocks were hardly better than sundials. Their metal parts rubbed together, and the weights powering their mechanism made them unreliable. Most clocks had just an hour hand. A minute hand was unnecessary because it never pointed the right way.

A spinning bar with weights at each end, called a foliot, controlled older clocks.

Precision pendulum

In 1656 Dutchman Christian Huygens (1629–1695) built the first working clock that used a pendulum to keep time. The pendulum alternately caught and released a cog-wheel. This spun other geared wheels, and eventually turned the hands. They went round at a constant speed because each of the pendulum's swings took exactly the same time. Huygens' clock could have a minute hand because it kept such good time.

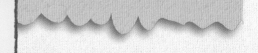

Huygens realised that doubling a pendulum's length makes it swing four times more slowly.

Bored in church

Huygens wasn't the first to think of using a pendulum to measure time. During a boring church service in 1582, Galileo (see page 8) started watching lamps swinging in Pisa Cathedral. He noticed that, no matter how far the lamp swung, it always took the same time to complete a full swing. Galileo and his son later built a pendulum clock, but never got it working.

Nickname

Difficult and argumentative even as a boy, Galileo was nicknamed "the Wrangler" by his school teachers.

3 seconds

3 seconds

The wider a pendulum swings, the faster it goes, but as long as its length does not change, each swing takes the same time.

PRINTING

The Renaissance brought a revolution in data storage. An amazing new device made it possible to share information faster than ever before. It needed no power supply, was completely portable, and it was made from renewable materials. Best of all it was 100 times cheaper than the system it replaced. This miracle device was the printed book.

Printers were IT specialists!

Slow work

Until the 15th century all books were made by hand. Monks sat and copied out every word, writing with a pen on vellum (calfskin). It was slow work, so there weren't many books, and they were amazingly expensive.

New technology

German goldsmith Johannes Gutenberg (c.1400–1468) had a brilliant idea: he invented a special mould, and made letters one-by-one from melted metal. He could arrange the letters into words, sentences and pages, print them, then separate them and rearrange them for the next page.

1
Gutenberg's workers cast type using the special mould he designed.

2
They poured molten metal into the mould.

3
Opening the mould released the letter. Casting took 10 seconds.

4
Letters were arranged in word order for printing.

Could you set that a little bigger?

Speedy printing

Gutenberg used three other inventions to print his specially moulded type. Paper, a Chinese invention new to Europe, was cheaper than vellum. The press (above) that squeezed together paper and letters was usually used to squeeze grapes for wine. And he borrowed the oily ink from painters (see pages 20–21). Gutenberg's invention spread rapidly across Europe. William Caxton (c.1422–1492) was the first printer in England.

Beautiful Bible

Among the first books that Gutenberg printed was a Bible (right). To make it look more like a traditional, hand-written book, Gutenberg left gaps in the type. Before binding the pages together, an artist decorated them with beautiful ornaments.

NAVIGATION

Are they going the right way?

For a 16th-century European, the world seemed to be growing at an alarming rate. In 1492 European mariners crossed the mid-Atlantic for the first time and discovered a continent or two. Thirty years later a ship sailed right around the world. Two new inventions – an instrument and a new kind of map – made voyages of discovery more adventurous and successful.

Finding the way

To navigate (find the way at sea) sailors used a lot of guess-work. They estimated how far they had sailed each day and drew the distances and directions on a chart (sea map) to work out where they had got to. However, this was none too accurate, and they often ended up on the rocks.

Sailors' solution

At noon each day the Sun reaches its highest point. How high it climbs depends on the season and on how far you are above or below the equator (Earth's waistline). So by accurately measuring the Sun's noon height navigators could work out how far they had sailed north or south. A new device – the cross-staff – made this measurement easy.

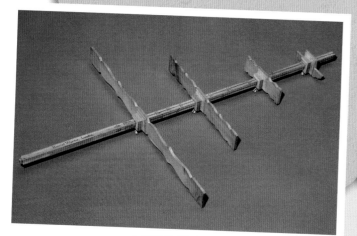

Better maps

In 1569 Flemish map-maker Gerardus Mercator (1512–1594) plotted the world on a new kind of map. For the first time, mariners could set their sailing direction straight from the map. It showed the quickest routes as straight lines, too: on earlier maps they were hard-to-follow curves.

Navigators gazed at the Sun and horizon across the top and bottom of the cross-staff's cross-bar, and read off their position from a scale on the long bar it slid along.

Using the right end helps!

Eastern ingenuity

European navigators learned their craft from the sailors of the East. The cross-staff was copied from an Arab instrument called the "kamal" and the magnetic compass (first used in the 13th century in Europe) was a Chinese invention.

THERMOMETER

Renaissance scientists knew that books could not tell them everything they wanted to know. To learn more they looked closely at the world around them. They took measurements so that they could record what they had seen. Measuring distance and weight was easy; clocks (see pages 12–13) made time measurement accurate. But temperature was no more than a vague idea until the end of the 16th century.

How hot is hot?

"How hot is it?" is something we ask ourselves daily before dressing, but nobody really thought about this question until the Renaissance. Then scientists began to notice that heat changes the speed of natural processes: most things go faster as they get warmer. They realised that it would be useful to measure the degree of hotness, and how it changed.

Galileo's invention

We don't know for sure who invented the first thermometer. What we do know is that around 1590, Galileo Galilei (see page 8) warmed a long air-filled tube and dipped the end in a bowl of water. As the room cooled down, the air inside the tube took up less space and the water level rose.

The changing water level gave Galileo a rough idea of the temperature in the room.

These 17th century medical thermometers from Florence are shaped like glass frogs. The ribbons were used to tie them to the patients' bodies.

Greater accuracy

Air thermometers are affected by the changing weather. Liquid-filled thermometers got round this problem. Scientists made the first, around 1654 in Italy. Though these instruments were an improvement, thermometers were not really useful until German physicist Daniel Fahrenheit (1686–1736) devised a standard scale so that it was possible to compare temperature.

Measuring air pressure

Baffled that pumps could not lift water from deep wells, Italian Gasparo Berti (c.1600–1643) tried an experiment in 1641. He fixed a water-filled pipe on a wall with its open end in a barrel of water. A vacuum (empty space) appeared at the top of the tube, some 10 m up. Though he didn't know it, Berti had measured air pressure: the weight of the Earth's atmosphere. This was what stopped *all* the water from flowing out of the tube.

We just have to wait for the pressure to change?!!

Changing air pressure affects weather patterns, so Berti's invention – which we now call a barometer – was useful for predicting the weather.

OIL PAINT

EUREKA!

With new paint, and a fresh way of drawing, Renaissance artists discovered a more lifelike way of recording the world. The people they painted look so real that you might think they are breathing. Scenes, like the one on the right, invite you to step into the picture. Artists would paint like this for 400 years – until the invention of photography in 1839 meant painters no longer needed to exactly copy what they saw.

Temperamental tempera

Most artists made paint from egg yolk and coloured chemicals. Called tempera, the paint had to be mixed to the right colour before use. Artists could not blend colours on the picture. It was difficult to paint in a lifelike way in tempera, and painters did not know how to make depth and distance look real in their pictures.

Oil for egg

In the early 15th century Dutch artist Jan van Eyck (c.1390–1441) replaced the egg in tempera paint with oil squeezed from plant seeds, and created "oil paint". With it he could blend colours on the painting. The paint was easy to work into fine detail. It dried to a hard surface. Van Eyck used oil paint to make pictures that are amazingly beautiful and lifelike, even today.

Van Eyck may have used himself as the subject of his 1433 *Man in a Red Turban* portrait.

In *School of Athens*, Italian artist Raphael (1483–1520) created a sense of depth by making the walls of the room close in towards the picture's centre.

Perspective

Paintings from the Renaissance look lifelike partly because artists began to use perspective. This is a special way of drawing how objects look, such as showing people in the distance smaller than those nearby. Italian artist Filippo Brunelleschi (1377–1446) was the first to work out how to use perspective, in the early 15th century.

Fantastic flax

Artists would have been stuck without the flax plant: its seeds provided the oil they used in their paint, and fibres of the stem were woven into the canvas they painted on.

WATER CLOSET

Even in the grandest Renaissance palace, it was hard to escape the smell of drains for there was no proper plumbing. All human waste ran into stinking pits or murky, smelly streams. In 1596 a royal courtier (noble servant) to England's Queen Elizabeth I aimed to clean up the mess with an invention that's now in every home.

Hgnggngnnn!!

Smelly sewage

Collected in buckets and pots, sewage – human bodily waste – smelled bad and attracted flies that spread disease. The wealthy used privies or garderobes, toilet seats hidden in castle or palace alcoves with streams or deep pits below them. Smelly serfs had to empty the pits with buckets and shovels when they overflowed.

Everything that dropped into a garderobe chute fell into the pit, moat or river below.

Streams washed sewage away – but they got stinky in summer when the water level fell.

Can you see where my poo goes?

Wonderful water closet

The queen's godson and courtier, John Harrington (c.1539–1613), suggested placing above a privy a tank of water, with a stopper in the pan to keep out smells. Emptying the tank flushed away the waste in the pan. He printed his description in a humorous essay called "The Metamorphosis of Ajax". The title was a bad joke: "a jakes" was a polite name for a privy.

Queen Elizabeth banned Harrington from Court for his poor taste in jokes but eventually forgave him. She installed one of his new-fangled water closets in her palace at Richmond.

Brilliant Bramah

Harrington's lavatory was not a great success. It required piped water, which was rare even in palaces. The first really successful water closet (right) was invented by another Englishman, Joseph Bramah (1748–1814), nearly 200 years later.

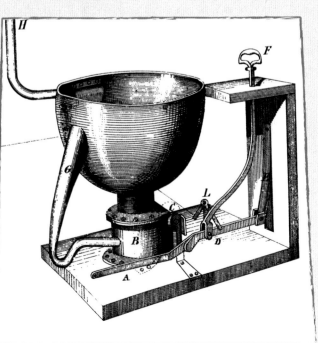

ARITHMETIC

What's XL minus XVII?

If you have problems with numbers, you're not alone. Many adults find even simple sums difficult. Arithmetic used to be even harder, with Roman numerals like X, V, I and C, and without signs like + and ÷. In the 15th century European people began using Arabic numerals...

1 2 3 4 5 6 7 8 9 0

...which made things much easier. Not long afterwards brainy Renaissance inventors thought up the symbols we still use for sums.

Number trouble

To understand why nobody could do sums, try adding XIX to VIII. Baffled? 19+8 is a lot easier, isn't it? Even adding up was so difficult that everyone used devices called counting frames. These were squares – rather like a chequer-board – or bars drawn on a table or a cloth. Moving counters on them helped to add up numbers. But a counting frame was no help for fractions (numbers smaller than 1).

This 1508 picture contrasts calculation on the old-fashioned counting frame (right) with modern sums using Arabic numbers (left).

24

Fractions made easy?

Arabic numbers allowed people to line up hundreds, tens and units in straight columns for adding up. The next step was to simplify fractions. Flemish mathematician Simon Stevin (c.1548–1620) found a way to do this, with decimal fractions, around 1586.

Stevin's fractions lacked a decimal point. Instead he showed the position of each digit in a circle. So this is how he would represent the number 123.45678

1 2 3 ⓪ 4 ① 5 ② 6 ③ 7 ④ 8

Phew! Separating the whole number from the fraction with a dot or comma began with printing (see page 14).

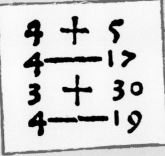

Plus and **minus** signs were first used in print in *Mercantile Arithmetic* by Johannes Widmann (c.1460–after 1498) in 1489.

✖ The **multiplication** symbol was the 1631 invention of English mathematician William Oughtred (1575–1660).

÷ This sign was first used to show division in 1659. Before that scholars called it an obelus, and used it to mark parts of a book they did not believe were true.

═ The **equals** sign was introduced by Welshman Robert Recorde (1510–1558) in 1557 in his book *The Whetstone of Witte.*

The Exchequer

The English government's finance department was called the Exchequer after the chequer-board counting frames its staff used for their sums. Some people still use the term to refer to financial matters.

KNITTING MACHINE

With just a couple of long, thick needles, a skilled knitter can turn yarn into soft, stretchy, ready-shaped clothes. However, knitting by hand is slow: making one silk sock can take days. A 17th century vicar who tired of his girlfriend's clicking needles decided to change this. His stocking frame invention was the first machine to make cloth from thread.

Slow work

Men's fashions were changing in the 16th century. Long robes were out of style. The short doublets (jackets) that replaced them showed off men's legs, and they wanted long knitted hose (stockings) to cover them up. Knitters made hose by hand, using their needles to form thousands of tiny loops in the thread, and building up the legs row by tedious, expensive row.

Espionage

The first recorded case of industrial spying began with the stocking frame. In 1656 Frenchman Jean Hindret made two dozen drawings of a machine in London, returned to France and recreated them there.

Speedy stockings

According to legend, William Lee took a fancy to a knitter, but she was too busy with her needles to pay him any attention. So he built a machine to knit her stockings and free up her hands. His first machine, built in 1589, used hooked needles to imitate the movements of hand knitters. It made four stitches to the centimetre and could only knit wool. But within nine years Lee had improved it so much that it could knit fine silk stockings. Lee failed to make money from his invention, but after his death his machines were widely copied. By 1664 there were 400 to 500 in London alone.

The clicking of his girfriend's knitting needles brought out the inventive spirit in William Lee, as depicted in this fanciful 19th-century engraving.

> Knit one, pearl one, knit two together. Oops! I think you dropped a stitch there, Bill.

William Lee

We don't know much about Lee. He probably lived in the village of Calverton, on the outskirts of Nottingham. When people showed little interest in his stocking frame in England, he took it to France, where he died in 1614 or 15. His brother James returned to England and brought eight "stocking frames" with him. With these he started the machine knitting industry in London.

DISTILLED ALCOHOL

Cheers!

Chemistry, and what we now call "chemicals", started in an unlikely way. Renaissance experimenters, called alchemists, were looking for miracle compounds such as the philosopher's stone. They believed this would turn to gold everything it touched. In the course of their searches they learned important ways of concentrating and purifying liquids and metals.

Alcoholic result

By boiling wine, Italian experimenters probably succeeded in preparing a crude form of purified alcohol around 1100. By the end of the 13th century, Arnau (or Arnald) de Villanova had made brandy – a delicious success, and not just for heavy drinkers. Distillation – the process he used – is a valuable way of separating mixtures of liquids. It is essential both to chemistry and many modern industrial processes.

Distillation

To make pure alcohol from wine, alchemists heated it in an alembic – a flask with a long neck (right). Wine is a mix of water and alcohol, and as the heat rose, the alcohol boiled before the water. Bubbling off as a vapour, it turned to liquid again on the flask's cool neck, and dripped into a collection bottle.

The dream solution

One of the alchemists' dreams was "alkahest", a universal solvent which would dissolve absolutely anything. (If they had succeeded, what would they have kept it in?) The alchemists were secretive, and their recipes read more like magic spells than laboratory notes, so we don't know how they planned to make alkahest.

Magic spell

Alchemists wrapped up their instructions in mysterious mumbo-jumbo, like this rhyme:

Dissolve the Fixt,
and make the Fixed fly,
The Flying fix,
and then live happily.

Most people thought of alchemists as greedy fools – or worse. They were nicknamed "puffers" because they seemed to be constantly squeezing bellows to fan the flames below their bubbling flasks.

GLOSSARY

alchemist Someone who mixes magic and science in search of an impossible goal, such as turning LEAD to gold.

alembic Glass bottle with a long neck, used by scientists and ALCHEMISTS.

Arabic numerals The numbers 1234567890 that we use today, that replaced ROMAN NUMERALS.

arithmetic Simple sums that add, subtract, multiply and divide numbers.

armour Strong (usually metal) clothes to protect warriors in battle.

atmosphere Mixture of gases that surrounds the Earth, making plant and animal life possible.

blacksmith Someone who heats metal in a fire and beats it into useful shapes.

catapult Device, usually powered by a spring, that hurls objects at an enemy or a hunted animal.

charcoal Black, smokeless fuel made by heating wood.

chequer-board Game board used for draughts or chess, painted with a regular pattern of black and white squares.

compass Magnetised needle that always points in the same direction, used by travellers to find their way.

cross-staff Simple device for measuring the height of the Sun or stars, used mostly by sailors to find their way.

decimal fraction Part of a number smaller than 1, and separated from that part greater than one by a dot called a decimal point.

distillation Separation using heat of a mixture of liquids that boil at different temperatures.

flax Plant with a blue flower grown for oil and for linen; the tough fibres of its stem.

garderobe Room containing a PRIVY, or the privy itself.

horizon Distant line where the sky meets the sea or land.

knitting Making fabric by tying many tiny loops in a thread using needles or a machine.

lead Heavy, grey-coloured metal of little value.

microscope Arrangement of one or more lenses, often held apart by a tube, to create enlarged views of tiny objects.

mould Specially-shaped container made to be filled with a liquid that hardens, copying exactly the shape of the inside of the container.

navigation Art and science of finding the way.

pendulum Swinging weight used in the past to control the speed of clocks.

perspective Special way of setting out a drawing or painting to give a sense of depth and distance on a flat picture.

privy Lavatory.

Renaissance Time of learning, experiment and discovery that began in Italy in the 14th century and lasted some 300 years.

Roman numerals Way of writing numbers, using the letters IVXLCDM, in use before ARABIC NUMERALS.

saltpetre White powdery chemical that, when mixed with many other substances and lit, makes them burn more quickly.

solvent Liquid that will melt a solid substance, and absorb it so completely that no trace remains, except perhaps its colour.

Stuart Name of the British royal family that ruled from 1603 when King James VI of Scotland became King James I of England and Wales. The last Stuart monarch, Queen Anne, died in 1714.

sulphur Yellow chemical that burns easily, giving off a choking smoke.

temperature Measure of hotness.

thermometer Device for measuring TEMPERATURE.

Tudor Name of the royal family of England and Wales from 1485 to 1603. Henry VIII and Elizabeth I were the two most famous Tudor monarchs.

vacuum Space from which all air has been removed.

vapour Gas into which liquids turn when heated until they boil.

vellum Thin sheet of calfskin, smoothed, dried and used for writing on before the invention of paper.

WEBSITES

All about Galileo
http://www.pbs.org/wgbh/nova/galileo/
Galileo's experiments: falling objects, projectiles, inclined planes, pendulum
http://www.pbs.org/wgbh/nova/galileo/experiments.html
Navigation
http://www.pbs.org/wgbh/nova/longitude/secrets.html
Galileo's microscope/telescope
http://brunelleschi.imss.fi.it/esplora/cannocchiale/dswmedia/storia/estoria2.html
All about Robert Hooke and his microscope
http://www.roberthooke.org.uk/

Note to parents and teachers:
Every effort has been made by the Publishers to ensure that the websites in this book are suitable for children, that they are of the highest educational value, and that they contain no inappropriate or offensive material. However, because of the nature of the Internet, it is impossible to guarantee that the contents of these sites will not be altered. We strongly advise that Internet access is supervised by a responsible adult.

INDEX

alchemists 28-29, 30

alcohol 28-29

Arabs 4, 6, 17, 24, 25, 30

arithmetic 24-25, 30

armour 6, 30

artists 20-21

barometers 19

Berti, Gasparo 19

books 5, 14-15, 18

Bramah, Joseph 23

Brunelleschi, Filippo 21

cannons 6, 7

castles 6, 7, 22

China 4, 6, 15, 17

clocks 5, 12-13, 18, 30

closets, water 22-23

Copernicus, Nikolaus 9

cross-staff 16, 17, 30

de Villanova, Arnau 28

distillation 28-29, 30

Elizabeth I 22, 23, 31

Fahrenheit, Daniel 19

firearms 6-7

Galilei, Galileo 8, 9, 13, 18, 31

glass, magnifying 10

Greece, ancient 4

gunpowder 6, 7

Gutenberg, Johannes 14, 15

Harrington, John 22, 23

Hooke, Robert 11, 31

Huygens, Christian 12, 13

India 4

Italy 4, 19, 21, 28, 30

knitting 26-27, 30

lavatories 22-23

Lee, William 27

Leeuwenhoek, Anton 10, 11

lenses 8-9, 10, 11, 30

Lippershey, Hans 8, 9

machines, knitting 26-27

maps 9, 16, 17

mariners 16-17

Mercator, Gerardus 17

microscopes 5, 10-11, 30, 31

navigation 16-17, 30, 31

numbers 24, 25, 30

opticians 8

Oughtred, William 25

paint, oil 15, 20-21

pendulums 12, 13, 30

perspective 21, 30

printing 4, 5, 14-15, 25

privies 22, 30

Raphael 21

Recorde, Robert 25

Rome, ancient 4

Stevin, Simon 25

telescopes 5, 8-9, 31

tempera 20

temperature 18-19, 30

thermometers 5, 18-19, 30

van Eyck, Jan 20

warfare 6-7

weapons 6

Widmann, Johannes 25